THE HOPI

BY LIZ SONNEBORN

CONSULTANT: TIM TOPPER,
CHEYENNE RIVER SIOUX

BLASTOFF! DISCOVERY

BELLWETHER MEDIA • MINNEAP

BLASTOFF! DISCOVERY

Blastoff! Discovery launches a new mission: reading to learn. Filled with facts and features, each book offers you an exciting new world to explore!

BLASTOFF! UNIVERSE

BLASTOFF! Beginners — GRADE K

BLASTOFF! READERS — GRADES 1-3

BLASTOFF! DISCOVERY — GRADE 4

Author's Statement of Positionality:
I am a white woman of German, Danish, Swedish, and Swiss descent. As such, I can claim no direct lived experience of being a Native American. In writing this book, however, I have tried to be an ally by relying on sources by Native American writers and authors whenever possible and have worked to let their voices guide its content.

This edition first published in 2024 by Bellwether Media, Inc.

Library of Congress Cataloging-in-Publication Data

Names: Sonneborn, Liz, author.
Title: The Hopi / by Liz Sonneborn.
Description: Minneapolis, MN : Bellwether Media, Inc. 2024. | Series: Blastoff! discovery : Native American nations | Includes bibliographical references and index. | Audience: Ages 7-13 | Audience: Grades 4-6 | Summary: "Engaging images accompany information about the Hopi people. The combination of high-interest subject matter and narrative text is intended for students in grades 3 through 8" – Provided by publisher.
Identifiers: LCCN 2023023106 (print) | LCCN 2023023107 (ebook) | ISBN 9798886874426 (library binding) | ISBN 9798886876307 (ebook)
Subjects: CYAC: Hopi Indians
Classification: LCC E99.H7 S66 2024 (print) | LCC E99.H7 (ebook) | DDC 979.100497458–dc23/eng/20230607
LC record available at https://lccn.loc.gov/2023023106
LC ebook record available at https://lccn.loc.gov/2023023107

Editor: Rebecca Sabelko   Series Designer: Andrea Schneider
Book Designer: Laura Sowers

Printed in the United States of America, North Mankato, MN.

TABLE OF CONTENTS

HISTORIC LANDMARK

HOPI HOUSE

NATIVE AMERICAN ARTS & CRAFTS
NAVAHO RUGS

The Hopi are a Native American nation. Their homeland is called *Hopitutskwa*. It is in northeastern Arizona. It includes 12 Hopi villages located on three **mesas**.

Ancestral Puebloan people inhabited the **Four Corners** region more than 1,000 years ago. The Hopi are one of several groups of **descendants** known today as the **Pueblos**. The name *Hopi* is short for *Hopisinom*. It means "people who live the correct way." The Hopi believe the creator Maasaw gave them their homeland. Maasaw told them to take good care of this special gift.

ARIZONA

ARIZONA

- 🟥 HOPI HOMELAND
- 🟦 SECOND MESA
- 🟨 FIRST MESA
- 🟪 THIRD MESA

MESA

OLD ORAIBI

The Hopi village of Old Oraibi was founded in about 1150 CE. It is the oldest continually occupied settlement in the United States.

Hopi land is located in a challenging climate. The land is very dry. It has no rivers or streams. It receives very little rain each year. The water the Hopi need to survive comes from springs and small amounts of rainwater.

The Hopi created a unique **culture** to survive these harsh conditions. The Hopi Way became central to their culture. The Hopi live in balance with nature. They are expected to respect one another. They believe community, love, and peace have allowed them to thrive in their desert homeland.

CORNFIELD

BASKETMAKING

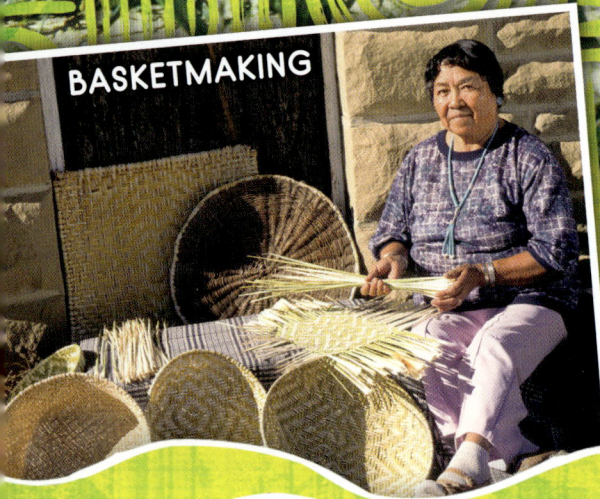

The Hopi's ancestors were skilled farmers. With the little rain they received, they grew corn, beans, squash, and cotton. Corn was their most important crop. They had about 50 ways of preparing this food. Women gathered wild nuts, roots, fruits, and seeds. Men occasionally hunted deer, rabbits, and other animals. They also raised turkeys for meat.

Ancestral Hopi crafted everything they needed by hand. Women made baskets from plant materials and pottery from clay. They also used plants to dye thread. Men wove the thread to make clothing and blankets.

HOPI RESOURCES

BLUE CORN →

PIKI BREAD

COTTON →

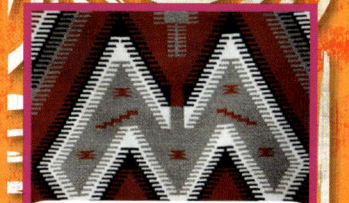

BLANKET

RABBITBRUSH →

BASKET

The Hopi's ancestors lived in villages with their **clan**. Their homes were called pueblos. Pueblos were made of stones and mud. They did not have windows or doors. People entered pueblos by climbing ladders to openings in the roofs. As families grew, rooms were often built on top. Some were five stories high.

Their ancestors also built **kivas**. These underground rooms had stone walls. Men gathered in kivas to perform religious **ceremonies**. The Hopi believed in spirits called **Katsinam**. Men wore masks to represent the spirits. The Hopi believed these ceremonies would bring rain and a good harvest. Some Hopi descendants honor Katsinam today.

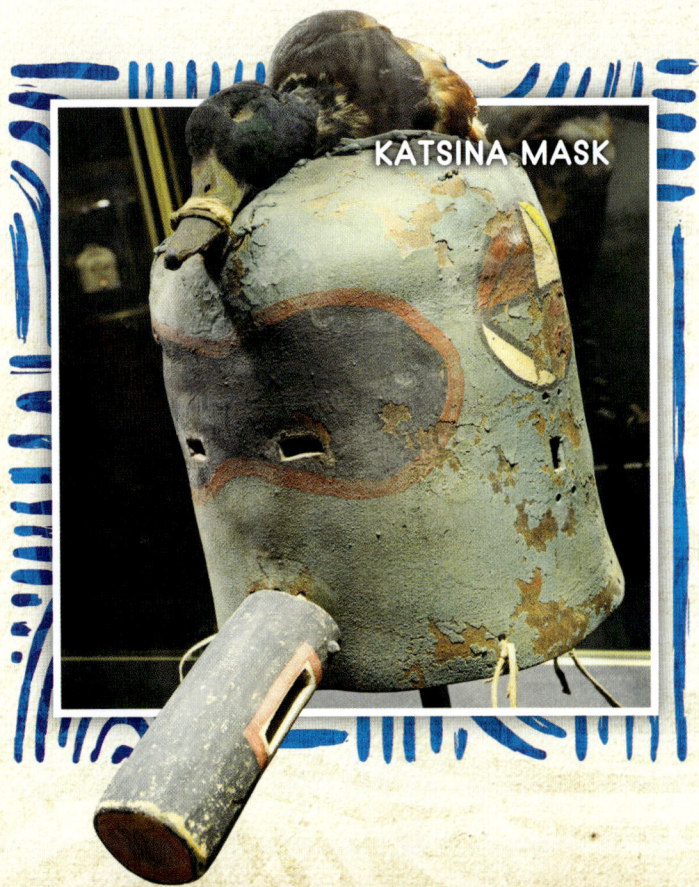

KATSINA MASK

A HOPI HAIRSTYLE

Young Hopi women traditionally wore their hair in two big curls near their ears. The hairstyle showed that a woman was ready to get married. The hairstyle is less common today.

KIVA ENTRANCE

MEMBERS OF THE FRANCISCO VÁZQUEZ DE CORONADO EXPEDITION

In 1540, Spaniards became the first Europeans to enter a Hopi village. They were members of the Francisco Vázquez de Coronado **expedition**. They were searching for gold. The Hopi did not want the Spaniards to enter their village. The Spaniards attacked. After, other Hopi villages were friendly to the Spaniards to keep their villages safe.

PO'PAY, PUEBLO LEADER WHO ORGANIZED THE PUEBLO REVOLT OF 1680

Over the next 140 years, more Spaniards arrived. They included Catholic priests. The priests pushed the Hopi to become Christians. The Hopi refused to abandon their religion. With other Pueblo peoples, they defeated their Spanish enemies in the Pueblo Revolt of 1680.

In 1821, Hopi land became part of Mexico. It became part of the United States in 1848. These events did not cause many changes for the Hopi. But in 1882, the U.S. government created the Hopi **Reservation**. This set new borders for Hopi land. The Hopi lost much of their land.

The U.S. government also tried to destroy Hopi culture. It wanted Hopi children to go to off-reservation schools. Many Hopi refused to give up their children. They fought the U.S. government again and again to keep their culture alive. Today, many Hopi continue to live by the Hopi Way.

FAMOUS HOPI

NAMPEYO

BIRTHDAY around 1860

DEATH 1942

FAMOUS FOR

One of the greatest Native American potters who decorated her work with designs copied from ancient Hopi pots

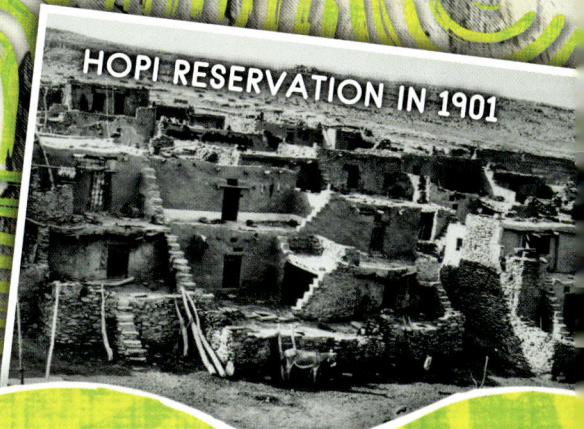

HOPI RESERVATION IN 1901

A CHAMPION

Tsökahovi Tewanima was one of many children forced to go to a U.S. government-run school. He used the ancient Hopi tradition of running to stay connected to his culture. Over time, he won many running awards, including an Olympic silver medal in 1912.

15

Today, the Hopi reservation stretches over more than 2,300 square miles (6,000 square kilometers). There are more than 18,000 members of the Hopi nation. About half of them live on the Hopi Reservation. Other members live in communities throughout the U.S. and in other countries.

The reservation's location and limited electricity and running water make jobs hard to find. People often have jobs with businesses off the reservation. Some Hopi practice **traditional** farming or raise sheep and cattle. Other Hopi sell traditional crafts. Members may also work for the tribal government.

ARIZONA

■ HOPI RESERVATION

HOPI ARTS AND CULTURE FAIR

The Hopi government is made up of a 22-member tribal **council**. The council carries out all business between the Hopi and the U.S. and Arizona governments.

Traditionally, each village works independently and has its own laws. Each is governed by the head of a clan. Because of this independence and tradition, many Hopi support their village laws more than the council.

GOVERNMENT OF THE HOPI NATION

LEGISLATIVE
- Hopi Tribal Council

ADMINISTRATIVE
- Tribal Chairman
- Vice Chairman

JUDICIAL
- Tribal Court

HOPI LEADERS MEETING WITH A MEMBER OF THE ARIZONA GOVERNMENT

A WINNING TEAM!

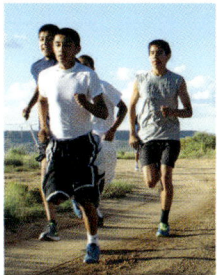

The Hopi Junior Senior High School has one of the best cross-country teams in Arizona!

19

HOPI ARTIST SELLING KATSINA DOLLS

ILLUSTRATION OF THE SNAKE DANCE

In some ways, the Hopi live much like other Americans. But many practice their ancient traditions. Some Hopi artists make traditional pots, baskets, and wooden Katsina dolls. Hopi craftspeople also work with silver. They make bracelets and buckles. Some artists earn money selling their work.

Religion is an important part of life for the Hopi. Many villages perform ceremonies that were practiced by their ancestors. For example, they perform the Snake Dance in August. Dancers release snakes to search for rain.

CELEBRATING HOPI CULTURE

Since 2010, the Hopi Arts and Cultural Festival has been held every year in Flagstaff, Arizona. The festival features art for sale and performances of traditional dances.

KATSINA DOLLS

Katsina dolls represent Katsinam. They are not toys. Hopi men carve the dolls. Young girls receive the dolls during ceremonies.

WHITE BUFFALO WARRIOR KATSINA

BLACK OGRE KATSINA

WOLF KATSINA

EAGLE KATSINA

Some Hopi live in pueblos. Today, pueblos usually have doors and windows. They may have indoor water and electricity.

HOPI HOUSE

Hopi House at Grand Canyon National Park is a recreated pueblo. Visitors can go inside to learn about these buildings and Hopi culture!

Many Native American languages are no longer spoken. But the Hopi have kept their language alive! Many Hopi speak both English and Hopi on the reservation. Traditionally, Hopi was only a spoken language. But in recent years, the tribe worked to develop a Hopi writing system. Young Hopi can now learn to speak, read, and write the Hopi language.

BLACK MESA COAL MINE

The Hopi may face many challenges in the future. The biggest is the threat to their water supply. For decades, a coal company operated two mines on Black Mesa. The mining damaged the land. It also pumped large amounts of water from the ground. The Hopi rely on this groundwater.

Climate change has caused a severe **drought** on their land. The lack of rain is threatening the way many Hopi live. Farmers are having trouble growing crops. Ranchers fear their animals will not have enough water to survive.

CORN CROP AFFECTED BY DROUGHT

Tribal leaders are working hard to solve the water problem. They pressure the U.S. government to fund new **wells** on the reservation. The Hopi government is building a pipeline that will bring fresh water into Hopi homes.

RANCHER PROVIDING WATER FOR CATTLE

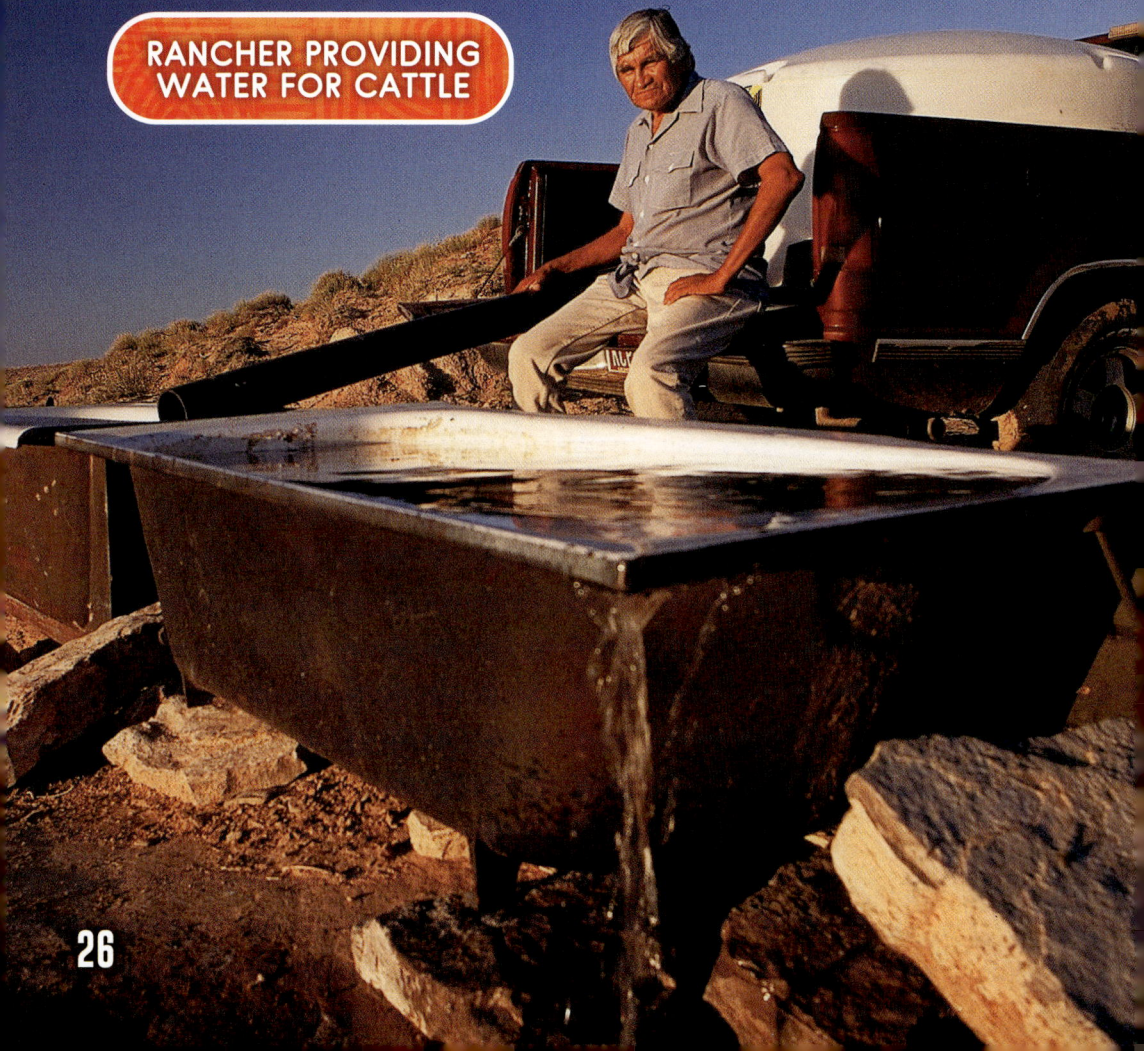

LITTLE COLORADO RIVER

The Hopi have taken their fight to court as well. They are seeking rights to the waters of the Little Colorado River. By taking up this challenge, the Hopi remain faithful caretakers of the land Maasaw gave them!

AROUND 1150

The Hopi village of Old Oraibi is founded

1540

Spanish men from the Coronado expedition become the first Europeans to meet the Hopi

1680

The Hopi participate in the Pueblo Revolt and drive Spaniards from their land

1848

Hopi land becomes part of the U.S.

1821

Hopi land becomes part of Mexico

1894
The U.S. government imprisons Hopi leaders for keeping children from government-run schools

2019
A coal company that began mining in the 1960s shuts down the Kayenta mine, but the company fails to return the land to its pre-mining condition

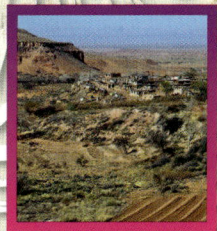

1936
The Hopi Tribal Council is established

2000 TO PRESENT
A severe drought threatens Hopi ranching and farming

1882
President Chester A. Arthur establishes the Hopi Reservation

GLOSSARY

Ancestral Puebloan—referring to maize, or corn, farmers who lived across the northern Southwest from the beginnings of agriculture until around 1540 CE

ceremonies—sets of actions performed in a particular way, often as part of religious worship

clan—a group of people who share a common ancestor

climate change—a human-caused change in Earth's weather due to warming temperatures

council—a group of people who meet to run a government

culture—the beliefs, arts, and ways of life in a place or society

descendants—people related to a person or group of people who lived at an earlier time

drought—an extended period of time with little to no rainfall

expedition—a journey taken for a specific reason, such as to explore a region

Four Corners—the area in the Southwestern United States where Colorado, New Mexico, Arizona, and Utah come together

Katsinam—spirits who live among the Hopi; one spirit is called a Katsina.

kivas—underground rooms where Hopi ceremonies are performed

mesas—high, flat-topped areas of land with steep sides

Pueblos—a group of peoples originating in the American Southwest, including the Hopi, the Zuni, and others

reservation—land set aside by the U.S. government for the forced removal of a Native American community from their original land

traditional—related to customs, ideas, or beliefs handed down from one generation to the next

wells—holes in the earth made to draw up water

TO LEARN MORE

AT THE LIBRARY

Bodden, Valerie. *Hopi*. Mankato, Minn.: Creative Education, 2018.

Grack, Rachel. *Arizona*. Minneapolis, Minn.: Bellwether Media, 2022.

O'Mara, John. *The Hopi*. New York, N.Y.: Enslow Publishing, 2022.

ON THE WEB

FACTSURFER

Factsurfer.com gives you a safe, fun way to find more information.

1. Go to www.factsurfer.com.

2. Enter "the Hopi" into the search box and click 🔍.

3. Select your book cover to see a list of related content.

INDEX